Starsai

Contents

Written by Helen Dineen

Collins

1 Welcome to the gallery

When you look at an artwork, what do you see? There's so much to look at, and the longer you look, the more details you might notice. If you spend a very long time looking, your imagination can start to take over, and stories or poems can start to unfold in your brain.

On the following pages, you'll discover
20 poems about the world around us, all
inspired by fascinating and important works
of art. Once you've read them all, perhaps
you'll be inspired to make some art or write
some poems of your own!

2 The natural world around us

Title: Sunflowers (1889)
Artist: Vincent van Gogh (The Netherlands)

Vincent van Gogh enjoyed experimenting with colour. To paint these sunflowers, he chose lots of different shades of yellow, which is a **warm colour**. They really stand out against the background, which is a **cool colour.**

Summer's begun

Yellows that burst with the warmth of the Sun,
A huge bunch of sunflowers brightens my day.
Their bright golden petals say, 'Summer's begun!'
(Yellows that burst with the warmth of the Sun.)

Raising their faces to greet everyone,
Their colours create an amazing display.
Yellows that burst with the warmth of the Sun,
A huge bunch of sunflowers brightens my day.

Which word choices make the poem feel 'warm' like the painting?

Cool | Warm

Title: Love of Winter (1914)
Artist: George Wesley Bellows (US)

George Wesley Bellows loved painting snow, so he was
very impatient when there was no snow in
New York in January 1914. Luckily for him, it did snow
in February, when he painted these skaters enjoying
the frozen pond. Focus on two or three of the people in
the scene and imagine what their story might be.

A city in the snow

In the shivering city that morning

There was silence in the streets. But then ...

Snow! Snow! came the cries from every window.

Suddenly the whole world was clothed in white, and

No one was thinking about work or school,

Only about the snow. Snow! At last!

We ran to the park, put on our skates,

Inched out onto the ice. Would it hold? Was it safe? Yes!

Now go! We whizzed across the pond, happy
    and laughing,

Gliding through a frozen, catch-your-breath world.

Read the first letter of each line.
Can you see the hidden message?

Hide and seek

"Let's play hide and seek," said Sun. "I've heard
　　　it's really fun!"
"I want to sneak behind you, Moon, and hide
　　　from everyone."
"But I'm so small," said Moon to Sun. "In fact,
　　　I've heard it said,
That you're 400 times as big ... so should
　　　I hide instead?"
"Oh, Moon," said Sun, "that's true, but then
　　　I'm really far away,
So when you move in front of me, you'll block out
　　　every ray."

So Moon sailed slowly through the sky until
　　　she covered Sun.
But when the day turned black as night, it
　　　frightened everyone.
"Oh no," said Sun, "they need to know I haven't
　　　gone forever!"
So Moon sailed on till Sun came back!
　　　"Thanks, Moon," said Sun. "You're clever!"

Title: The Eclipse (1970)
Artist: Alma Thomas (US)

Alma Thomas's art often explored a space theme. Here, she was inspired by a **total solar eclipse** that was visible from the US in 1970. If you look closely, you will see that the painting is made of bold, wide brush strokes. What effect do you think this has?

Title: Paris Street; Rainy Day (1877)
Artist: Gustave Caillebotte (France)

This image is small on the page, but in the real painting the people walking towards you are life-size! Viewing it in an art **gallery** makes you feel like you are almost in the scene with them.

Imagine you are standing in this street. How do you feel? Serious, gloomy, energetic or something else?

A rainy day adventure

It's raining, it's pouring,
But staying inside is boring.

So grab your umbrella and let's go outside!
We'll roam through the city, explore far and wide.
We'll stroll down the **boulevards,** sidestep each puddle,
As everyone else hurries home in a huddle.

And when we get tired and our feet start to ache,
We'll find a café for hot chocolate and cake.

Title: Under the Wave off Kanagawa
(also called The Great Wave) (1830–1833)
Artist: Katsushika Hokusai (Japan)

Katsushika Hokusai's **seascape** isn't a painting. It was printed by rolling inks onto specially carved wood and pressing the wood onto paper.

Around 8,000 prints were made, but most of them have been lost because people didn't think they were very valuable at the time. Now, his giant wave is one of the most famous images in the world.

The blue wave

The blue wave keeps rising,
Up, up, up it goes.

It almost looks alive!
Like a huge, powerful creature
About to leap and roar.

It reaches out with white fingers of foam,
Ready to snatch the boats below.

The sailors shout out to each other,
They feel the dangerous breath of the wave
on their necks.

But they keep rowing,
On, on, on they go.

Can you spot Mount Fuji, a famous Japanese mountain, in the background?

Title: The Starry Night (1889)
Artist: Vincent van Gogh (The Netherlands)

One morning, Vincent van Gogh woke up very early, while it was still dark. He looked out of his window and saw the Moon, the planet Venus and the stars. They inspired him to paint this beautiful painting of the French **landscape** at night.

Can you find the Moon and Venus in the painting?

Starsailing

I saw a clear and starry night.
The whole world had a special glow.
The twinkling stars hung high above
The sleeping village far below.

The sky looked just like ocean waves,
It seemed as if the stars could float.
I wondered what it would be like
To sail across it in a boat.

I also saw the crescent Moon
And Venus ringed with dazzling white.
I sat for hours, just gazing at
The beauty of that starry night.

3 Animals in action

Title: The Goldfish (1925)
Artist: Paul Klee (Switzerland, Germany)

What a mysterious fish! There is a strong **contrast** between the bright yellow fish and the dark blue-black background. This really makes the fish stand out, suggesting that it's very different from the others.

The visitor

The river was deep, large and unknown.
The river was silent and still.
The little fish played, they dawdled and dived,
Just minding their business, until ...

A new fish arrived, a fish all alone,
And this fish was silent and still.
Its scales seemed to glow with a mythical light
That lit up the darkness, until ...

The little fish fled, they darted away,
And hid round the next river bend.
If only they'd stayed, they might have found out
The big fish just needed a friend.

How would you explain the mystery of the goldfish?

Title: A reclining tiger (late 1800s/early 1900s)
Artist: Géza Vastagh (Hungary)

Géza Vastagh loved painting big cats, especially lions and tigers. Here, he has used brush strokes to cleverly show the soft **texture** and the stripy pattern of the tiger's fur. What do you think the tiger is thinking?

Tiger!

Tail-swishing
Stream-swimming
Tree-climbing
Tiger.

Shade-finding
Limb-stretching
Day-snoozing
Tiger.

Eye-flashing
Ear-twitching
Scent-sniffing
Tiger.

Night-hunting
Prey-chasing
Meat-chomping
Tiger.

Teeth-baring
Roar-making
Ground-shaking
TIGER!

Fabulous falcons

Falcons fly high, they swoop and they soar, they scan the sky, and then with a whoooooooooooooooooooooooosh! of their wings they dive down and snatch their prey.

Title: "Horus of Gold" (4th century BCE)
Artist: unknown (Egypt)

Falcons were special birds in Ancient Egypt.
In art, they were used to represent Horus,
the Ancient Egyptian Sun god and the god of kings.
Falcons are very strong, quick and elegant.
They can dive through the sky at nearly
400 kilometres per hour! What adjectives would
you use to describe these birds?

Title: Cat Watching a Spider (1888–1892)
Artist: Ōide Tōkō (Japan)

This painting uses lots of **muted colours**, except for the cat's beautiful, bright scarf. It almost feels like time has stopped in this scene. Do you think the spider has seen the cat?

My cat

My cat is a hunter
Stalking its prey
Eyes watching
Ears listening

My cat is a statue
Frozen in time
Body crouching
Muscles tensing

My cat is waiting,
waiting,
waiting.

What do you think the cat is waiting for?

Title: Molly Wales Fobes or "Lady with Her Pets" (1790)
Artist: Rufus Hathaway (US)

Portraits can often tell us a lot about the person being painted. This lady's family was interested in studying animals. Animals were also a **symbol** of her beauty and caring nature. She is surrounded by three types of animal. Can you identify them? Are any of them surprising?

Incredible pets

Some of us want hamsters,
Some of us want dogs,
Some of us want stick insects or terrapins or frogs.

Some of us want ferrets,
Some of us want cats,
Some of us want angelfish or butterflies or rats.

Some of us want rabbits,
Some of us want moths,
Some of us want porcupines or polar bears or sloths.

Some of us want songbirds,
Some of us want snails,
Some of us want crocodiles or elephants or whales.

What would you choose to include in your own portrait?

4 People with a story to tell

My grandpa

Look! There's my grandpa.
He's working in the garden again.
He'll be there all day, you know.
He'll:
- dig over the soil
- scoop up the leaves
- tidy the daffodils
- carefully move a snail or two.

He's making sure his garden grows just right.

But once the Sun starts to set, he'll come inside.
And then, he'll:
- make me his special soup
- fill up my glass with water
- give me the biggest of hugs
- read me a bedtime story.

Do you know what?
I think he might be making sure I grow just right too.

Title: The Gardener (1882–1883)
Artist: Georges Seurat (France)

Georges Seurat was skilled at painting light
and shadows. He used dabs of paint in white,
yellow and green to show how the Sun shone on
this garden. If you look closely, you can see the
small individual brush strokes.

Title: Girl with a Pearl Earring (**circa** 1665)
Artist: Johannes Vermeer (The Netherlands)

Although this portrait is one of the most famous paintings in the world, nobody knows who the **model** was, or anything about her life.
What questions would you ask her?

What's her story?

I wonder what she's thinking?
I wonder what she'd say?
I wonder if she'd like to see what life is like today?
I wonder what her life was like in 1665?
A world 400 years ago! That's when she was alive.
I want to ask her questions: Are you happy?
      Are you sad?
Do you go to work or school, and is it good or is it bad?
Do you often sit for paintings? Is it boring, is it fun?
Did you ever guess your painting would be seen
      by everyone?
There's so much more I'd like to ask, but she lived
      long ago.
So she will stay a mystery – and I will never know.

Title: Ancient Storyteller (1940)
Artist: Amrita Sher-Gil (India, Hungary)

Amrita Sher-Gil liked to paint scenes of everyday life. In India, there is an important tradition of spoken storytelling. Many traditional tales have been passed down from generation to generation this way. Why do you think Sher-Gil might have wanted to paint a storyteller and his audience?

The storyteller

I pull each word from deep inside my mind
Where precious stories from our past are kept,
And as I tell each story, we are joined
To everyone from generations gone.

The children love to listen, though they've heard
These stories many, many times before,
I'll never tire of sharing ancient tales
And hope, one day, they too will pass them on.

My day at work

Come and spend the day with me!

I work in this huge factory.

We start each day at half past eight

(That's when they open up the gates)

I hear the sound of drumming feet,

As crowds pour in from every street.

Still more arrive from train and bus

And hurry in with all of us.

My job's on the production line

With Sam and Rav and Caroline.

Our team is such a friendly bunch!

We work all day (except for lunch)

And then at five, our day's complete

And crowds stream out to every street.

Title: Going to Work (1943)
Artist: LS Lowry (UK)

LS Lowry is famous for painting industrial landscapes and city scenes. The people he included are often called 'matchstick' people because of their shape: long and thin. In this painting, they are going to work in factories and offices in Manchester during the Second World War. What sounds can you 'hear' when you look at this scene?

Title: Bwanga bwa Cibola – Mother-and-Child Figure (circa 1850–1899)
Artist: unknown, Luluwa culture (Democratic Republic of Congo)

This precious figure has been carefully carved from wood. It shows a mother holding her tiny baby in her arms. She is holding it very close to her, to protect it. Look at the mother's face. How do you think she is feeling?

A mother's love

Kind mother, patient mother,
With a love that's deep.
Tired mother, weary mother,
Rocks her child to sleep.

Warm mother, clever mother,
With the biggest heart.
Strong mother, brave mother,
She's a work of art.

Title: In the Classroom (1886)
Artist: Paul Louis Martin des Amoignes (France)

These boys lived a long time ago, but the painting almost looks like a modern photograph. This is because Paul Louis Martin des Amoignes was part of a **movement** called **Naturalism**, which tried to show everyday life exactly as it was. Which details are similar to or different from your school?

How I feel about school

You won't change my mind!
School is boring
So don't try to convince me that
We can learn incredible things in this classroom
Because every single day
I'd rather be anywhere else
And I'll never agree with people who say
My teacher is amazing
Instead, I feel like shouting from the rooftops that
This lesson is almost over
But I hate that
There's still ten minutes left ...

Now read the poem from bottom to top, starting with the last line. Which version do you think each boy in the painting would agree with?

Title: Two Sisters (On the Terrace) (1881)
Artist: Pierre-Auguste Renoir (France)

The title of this portrait is *Two Sisters* but in fact
the two girls were not related at all! The older girl
was called Jeanne. She later became an actor.
The identity of the younger girl, however, is
a mystery. What do you think is in the girls' basket?

My family

Hi! My name is Lucy, and my older sister's Jeanne.
I'm very nearly seven, but my sister's seventeen.
She listens to me read and sometimes
      teaches me to sew.
She wants to work in fashion and she makes
      a lot of clothes.

My brother's even older! Tom is almost twenty-two.
He moved out not that long ago and
      works at City Zoo.
He comes home maybe once a month and brings me
      books and cakes,
And tells me lots of facts about alpacas,
      bats and snakes.

5 An explosion of colour

Title: Colour Study: Squares with Concentric Circles (1913)
Artist: Wassily Kandinsky (Russia)

Wassily Kandinsky loved using colour, shapes and lines in his work. He painted these circles to experiment with different colour combinations. Which colours do you think go well together? Are there any combinations that you don't like?

Everything starts from a dot

First, take a big sheet of paper.

Use a pencil and ruler to divide it into squares.

Next, grab some paints. Red, blue and yellow will do.

You can mix them to make other colours.

Using a brush, paint a big colourful dot in the middle of a square.

Everything starts from a dot!

Dollop some more dots in the other squares.

Now, paint circles around your dots,

more and more ... and more! No need to be perfect.

Messy is just fine.

When your circles almost fill each square, colour in any gaps.

And ... you're done!

Step back and take a look at your amazing work.

Wassily Kandinsky famously said, "Everything starts from a dot." What does this mean to you?

Look up!

We stamp our feet and shiver in the cold November air.

*Look up! Look up! The fireworks! Can you see them?
Over there!*

Whizz

Bang

Whoosh!

Zip

Pop

Zoom!

Crackle

Crackle

Shimmer

Shimmer

Whizz

Bang

Boom!

They're colourful and beautiful and sparkling so bright,

Amazing rockets shoot and soar across the
pitch-black night.

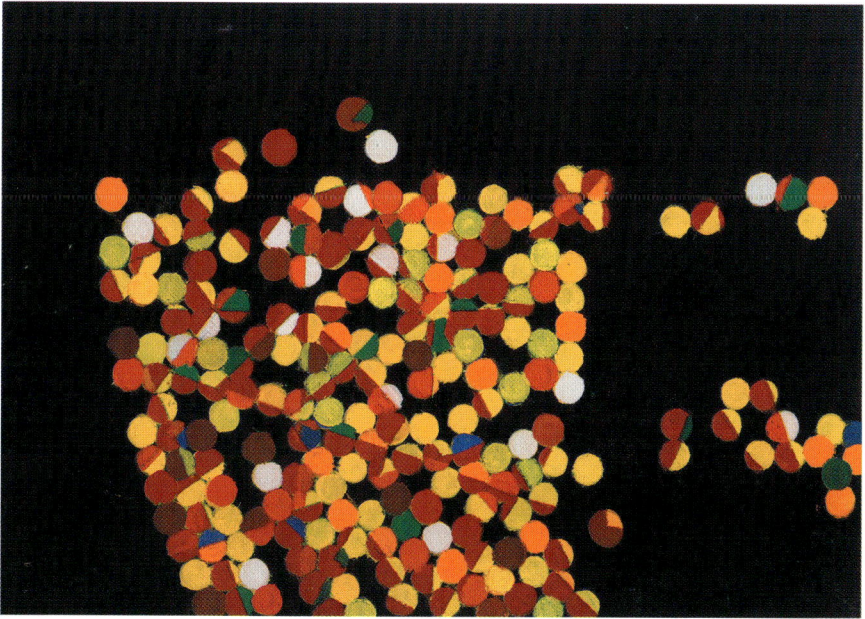

Title: Fireworks (1972)
Artist: Wilhelmina Barns-Graham (UK)

Wilhelmina Barns-Graham has used a black background for her painting. This really helps to make the fireworks stand out! Can you 'hear' them crackle and pop? Has Barns-Graham used warm or cool colours? Why do you think that is?

Glossary

boulevards	wide avenues or streets in a city
circa	around (in relation to a year)
contrast	a strong difference between two things, such as colours
cool colour	blue, green or purple, or similar colours
gallery	a room or building where art is displayed
landscape	a scene showing an area of land, such as mountains or fields
model	a person an artist draws or paints
movement	a group of artists working in a certain style at a particular time
muted colours	soft, calming colours, not bright
Naturalism	aiming to show the subject of the artwork exactly as it is
portraits	artworks that focus on a person
seascape	a scene set on or next to the sea
symbol	a thing used to represent a different idea, theme or feeling

texture	the way a surface or object feels
total solar eclipse	when the Moon completely covers the Sun, blocking any light from reaching Earth
warm colour	red, orange or yellow, or similar colours

Index

Timeline

4th century BCE

1665

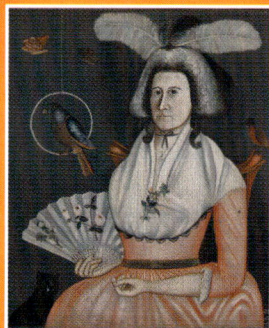

1790

1886

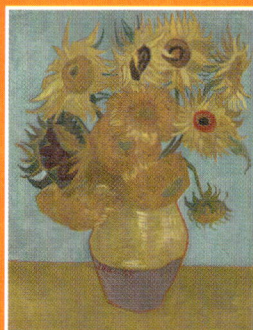

1889

1830

1850

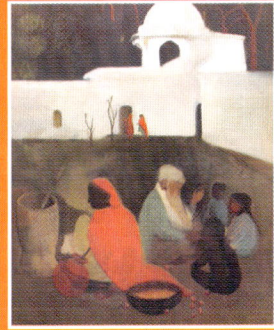

1913

1925

1940

❖ Ideas for reading ❖

Written by Gill Matthews
Primary Literacy Consultant

Reading objectives:

- be introduced to non-fiction books that are structured in different ways
- discuss and clarify the meanings of words
- answer and ask questions
- explain and discuss their understanding of books, poems and other material, both those that they listen to and those that they read for themselves

Spoken language objectives:

- participate in discussions
- speculate, hypothesise, imagine and explore ideas through talk
- ask relevant questions

Curriculum links: Art and design: Evaluate and analyse creative works using the language of art, craft and design; Know about great artists, craft makers and designers, and understand the historical and cultural development of their art forms

Word count: 2987

Interest words: shades, details, shapes, combinations, background

Resources: paper, pencils and crayons

Build a context for reading

- Ask children to look closely at the front cover of the book and to read the title. Discuss how the title could be linked to the painting on the cover.
- Read the back cover blurb. Discuss how poetry and paintings could be linked.
- Point out that this is a book that brings together information about paintings (non-fiction) with poetry. Explore children's knowledge of the typical features of non-fiction. Give them a few minutes to flick through the book to see which features this book has e.g. contents, glossary, index.
- Discuss the purpose and organisation of those features.